And No Birds Sing

by Kyle McHale

The sedge has wither'd from the lake
and no birds sing.

La Belle Dame Sans Merci
John Keats (1795-1821)

And No Birds Sing

Kyle McHale © 2017

Published by Dempsey & Windle

15 Rosetrees
Guildford
Surrey
GU1 2HS
01483 571164

dempseyandwindle.co.uk

A CIP record for this book can be obtained from the British Library.

ISBN: 978-1-907435-42-3

Cover picture: *Refuge* (1930) by Paul Klee

Printed in the United Kingdom by BookPrintingUK,
Remus House, Coltsfoot Drive, Woodston, Peterborough, PE2 9BF

To friends, family and loved ones.
Thank you for living and sharing this life.

Contents

Welcome to the Dying Season

You said, *I'm not scared of dying.*
I'm scared of the unknown, the feeling
I used to get before I entered a firefight.
Bub, there are firefights I had no business
walking out of.

I said, *Well, Dad, it's all unknown.*

I'll fight it. And I guess the rest
is up to the Great Maker.

So the last six months began in spring;
a huge snow-drift remained by the hospital
parking garage, melting slowly; it had
less time than you did,
this all is a matter of time.

The hospital staff made you wheel
out to the road to smoke your cigarettes,
your old Vietnam veteran ass hanging
out in the breeze of your hospital gown
for drivers to see as they passed by;
you have to laugh a little.

Summer came.
It was hard for us.

We took you to the woods one last time
and I knew you could move on then.
You spoke in firelight to others, like
the old ways and I had never seen
listening like that, every word said,
but more so, what had been unsaid
and left in roaring firelight.
So you died on the last day of summer,
so the dying season began.

Who's to measure this life in years?
You were here for twenty-five of mine;
I wish I had measured our time
in seasons instead; that would
have been ninety-nine.

You left me to go through
my favorite season alone.
Perhaps it had to be that way,

the cooling off,
the shutting down,
the dying land,
the falling colors;

now I hope to measure
time in seconds only,
a thousand lifetimes left
before I see you,
and in seconds I know now
a single bird song,
a single ray of sun,
a single piece of frost,
on a single apple in
cold morning mist
and the second's delay
of pre-sunrise light,
that most people never stop and see,
welcome the seconds,
welcome, welcome to the dying season.

Boat Trip

In the undone we live, imagine,
fester heavy in the dream pursuits
we let slip away,

sitting on the beach wishing to
always go to the other side
across anything,

get in that boat and if the sharks
eat you at least you'll be a hero,
though in a dumb kind of way,

but the old timers who tell your
tale will have to answer for
themselves why they never left,

and who will be dumb when they
have to say
why you died alone?

At the Pond

At the pond with Gramps I
did not know what I was
becoming, I thought it would
be like that forever, that I
could always catch bullfrogs
and fire-bellied newts with
my small hands, Gramps
guiding me over my shoulder.

Years later the pond changed,
I caught catfish and large-mouth bass.
My fishing line connected me to the web
of every living thing, to the pond
Gramps fished on his childhood
farm. Gramps confined to a chair,
I could still march up the hill and
tell him the day's fishing stories.
I thought it would be like that forever.

That I crossed that pond in every way,
in a small rowboat that leaked,
by foot around its edges, by a
young brave swim,
was proof of it all,
of early earth
when life began, to
more developed creatures to
a place, a pond teeming with
all that makes life pleasant.

In his eyes I from boy to young man,
some potential he saw in youth,
in my eyes Gramps from old to older,
strong to frail, life to wisdom to rest.

To know Gramps gave time as
if he were the pond, as if he had
an infinite mound of sand in some
hidden room somewhere that he
could fill up the hour glass with,
fill up the pond with creatures to
fish for after he had gone, fill up
my head with infinite cherished
gifts, birds and frogs and snakes and fish.

The Wood Carver

Those colors I remember could not
have been from any natural thing,
Gramps claiming, *Nothing in nature is perfect.*
Downstairs in his workshop, his new
retired hobby, carving ducks out of Tupelo wood.
Shipped up from Florida, he would say,
You smell that Kyle? It's sweet smellin wood
you see, soft, from the swamps, good for carving.

His hands rough with life would delicately
start shaping his vision, whatever bird filled
his mind first, perhaps the ducks that swam
around his farm's pond when he was a boy,
his love of all animals, so why birds, why ducks?

That smell of burning wood in the workshop,
sweetness that still sits somewhere in my brain,
wood burning every detailed line on every
little feather, every angle getting the time it deserved,
until the duck became as alive as
a black and white photograph,
until he was ready to go color-
mixing a thousand times, until
his memories and his eyes agreed upon
a certain type of green or red or blue,

the metallic green of a mallard's head,
his finest achievement, enough to win
a blue ribbon at the county fair.

When one of his ducks took second or third
place it was known, *That first place bird
was a parrot with a damned bright yellow beak,
you just don't see that in nature, eehhhhhh,
judges are a bunch of rednecks from the valley,
don't know their asses from their elbows,
a bunch of damned yo-yos.*

He let me carve a small fish into a plaque once;
I ruined the tail fin, completely uneven,
That's OK Kyle, nothing in nature is perfect.
His cabin became a wooden zoo, ducks, other
birds, even fish swam around the rooms.
His heart full with his new hobby, Gramps
began to create wooden gifts for people.
The mallard drake he carved, burned, and painted
for me sits on a small wooden table,
that shiny green head, those blue-tipped wings,
more real than not, out of nature,
life-keeping in the dust it collects,
a frozen moment of everything,
perfect.

Front Step

When you arrive here in the rain
at my door, flawed in every way,
like everything I have owned or known,
flawed like us, cracked
like the foundations
we always seemed to build on
or the old front steps
we sat and drank on,
know that my front step is dry, warm,
ny door, like yours, is always open.

My old friends, we have shared many
drinks together and all that follows that.
If you still drink, I will fill up a glass
for you, raise mine high to greet you,
keep my front step open for you.
Please knock; even if the step
seems in ruin, a friend is there.

Burdens arise but they are never
in the form of drifting friends.

Curled Up

Curled up like old paper that
listed who came, from where
and when, all from the British Isles;
Wales, Ireland, Scotland, England.

Curled up like your old fingers,
that knitted us hats and slippers,
baked us cakes and cookies
and wrote warm messages in cards.

Curled up like the frail dreams
of those before, like the crisping
and crunching of old paper and leaves.

Curled up fingers like now,
around this ink and pen
when those before me huddled
at night during war to write
to those they loved before
I knew the world,
before I knew why I could
curl up warm at night,
safely sleep under the spells
scrolled by the fingers of autumn.

Stone Ribcage

Cupped in hand
a tiny bird's ribcage,
hollowed out,
a holy shell,
a few feather tufts
of life clinging to
what has gone.

The corners of this old
stone house hold love
somewhere
deep in the smooth
river-stones that lay
once in a happier place,

where fire warmed the rooms
of those safely sleeping.

Now the smoke seems to
drift around cold, only
to fill the lungs with
toxic fumes,
covering up the
love-stones in some
corner of some wall
and those left are no more than
feather-tufts clinging
in the wind and smoke
of a dead stone-bird's-ribcage.

The Blessing

Yesterday, I asked Laura's father
if I could marry her.
The day before and today
I saw rainbows;
I don't know what it means
in folklore but I'll take it
as a blessing,

Arched light over an old pub
in soft rain,
a few early evening robins
perched on the old roof,
a tranquil river keeping
secrets, and canal boats
that haven't moved for years,
in the angels' light,
softly dark,
softly light,
and a gold sliver
through friendly clouds
to end the day with a pink
tinge of natural candlelight.

I feel that autumn love
is on my side tonight.

Feeding the Animals

He couldn't sleep when
the animals were cold.
He knew the cold;
he knew the twisting knot
of going hungry
and the shuffling around
a camp like a
stick with legs.

Food became love:
his first wife died from
being over fed;
the deer were fat,
the turkeys too;
the dog even died
because we could not
eat all the leftovers
at meals.

When my mother was
going through the
divorce we ate fast food;
she was sad
and Happy Meals
made us happy.

We drank in private
but family time was food;
we ignored the issues in
the room: we ate them.
We ignored a lot of things.

Some of us died fat,
some of us died drunk,
some of us died sad.

We were all fed to be happy kids,
yet still we all became
crying men.

Between Buildings

As children we sought new hiding spots,
explored between houses, down paths,
under benches, through gaps in stone
walls and wooden fences, between
churches and tombstones and stained
glass in day light, sheds and gardens,
between buildings where strange, unseen
flowering vines hid in summer,
unpicked fruit trees blossomed and no one
noticed us, they never even looked,
they wouldn't have seen us
even if they tried,
even if they wanted to;
we had found the gaps to dance and sing in.

Peace in cities is in the wanderings
down side streets, alleys that lessen
the humming of the universe, where
graffiti can be appreciated and life can
be seen, felt in every window and on every
balcony, families sharing meals and someone
sitting out enjoying a beer and a smoke,
listening to the radio,
the urban plants do their best to clean the air
between buildings, the only stillness left.

Then there was us in Venice;
it is better than they say,
being lost in Venice means anything
you wish it to mean, there is no
childhood pretending needed.

The apartment we stayed in had a
neglected courtyard between four walls:
over-grown, cracked, forgotten, rusty-barred
balconies and ripened vines; tattered drying
clothes out on lines; the sun was trying
to touch it all, the climbing plants grew
where it was possible to grow in the gaps
between brick rows out of the beautiful
sinking city and rose like
our heart-fires rose.

At night, to look between buildings
into that city-silvered sky, chasing
what can't be seen: perhaps
a star or a place, some dream in the gaps
that dreamers dance between
what's been built and what's been felt,
in the veins of the city, or of the heart,
in the center, in between it all at night,
there is always hope for a small flow
of faint warm light.

Old Stone Wall

We played in those woods by the creek
on the other side of that neglected
old stone wall, built by hand,
farmers' hands a century or so ago,
nothing ancient, except the rocks
smoothed over by water, flipped over
by us to look for worms,
beetles and salamanders.
We were unsupervised,
allowed to be children with imagination,
to carve spears and make arrowheads,
protect our sacred wall from
neighboring tribes.
You all knew the woods would not kill us,
that the old stone wall would keep us safe:
you had all been to real war,
built your own stone walls around your hearts,
prayed war would never find us in the woods.

We did not know of the walls you
crouched behind with dying friends and bullets,
we knew the walls you built with memories,
with long, lonely stares and
bad dreams you did not share.

You have all crossed that final wall;
looking back,

      I have never been so thankful
          to you imperfect men
               who let us climb over
                    and play on the warm,
                        loving side of those
                            old stone walls
                               around your hearts.

That is No Place for Birds

After heavy loss, sorrow-stricken streets,
crushed towns, empty houses,
that is no place for birds
but still a robin sits and sings on the gate,
through the rainy kitchen window,
knows you're sad,
and waits.

After heavy loss, torn, convoluted earth,
shell-holes, blood-stained muddy puddles,
lost young souls.
It has been one hundred years since the Somme.
That was no place for birds
but they found perches,
even on shattered trees;
even if the worms they ate
crawled out of the eye-sockets of the dead,
they were fed, singing still,
knew the sadness in the air, and waited.

In my dreams
I cannot control
a shock of living,
re-living in a
make-believe dream world,
a make-believe real world
that is no place for birds,
until a giant eagle appears,
tucks me under his wing
to rest on his warm breast,
to keep the bad noises out.
He knows my sadness.
He lets me sing
and waits.

The Trees are With Me

For if I could endure it all
to make it through this dreadful fall,
when my father left with the leaves
to catch and glide that color breeze,

I may see what my father's done,
taking pride as his oldest son,
that clarity in autumn light,
that calling out, those pleasant nights,

where I can send a fire out
of whipping tails sending up,
into the space my father went,
warming all that pain he felt,

and gently touching life's great web,
listening to what those trees said:

We have your father, he is here,
we send his heart out everywhere.

Let us touch you with our grace,
your father's heart's in natural place,
when you gaze towards heaven's glow,
when you are lost and want to know,

the Great Maker has taken care
of his brave spirit in the air,
for you know what type he was,
part wolf, part bear, eagle and dove,

part sea and land, part guiding hands,
part father, brother, teacher, friend.
You see, we needed him so much,
so that his soul at last could touch

all it earned in a mortal life,
to never feel a lonely night,
but you must stay and find that out,
seek guidance in the spirit clouds,

then closer to the heart you'll be,
yours and his beat beautifully.

Dear Trees, I'm still travelling lost,
I stand where place and time do cross,
I'll stay with fire close to ground,
I'll stay lost and hope I'm found

by where my father's heart has touched,
by how he filled my life with love.
enjoy his heart in autumn moon,
I'll see him again but no time soon.

Be at peace with everything,
I'll look for you when Eagles sing.

Blood-Maple

Spilled out on autumn ground
pooled deep,
bright red maple leaves:
a blood-pond where
things go to die

and farther north somewhere,
the frothy blood-mouth of
a white mother-wolf shines
bright in the snow;
she shows her teeth,
licks her lips
and takes in life
from a blood-pool;
howls a hopeless call.

There must be a place where
I can dip my face in,
cry deeply, scream a
hopeless scream like
screaming under water
or howling into arctic air,
a place I can emerge with a
mad, frothy blood-mouth,
refreshed, nourished
when all is dying
and the lonely live
at the edge of the setting sun
to keep warm
in a forgotten place.

Coward

My old friend's wife had a black eye;
he and I went back to youth,
I thought, *He's still just a nice guy.*
She brushed it off when asked the truth.
A lot of people knew it then
but I never asked him to know,
so I let it pass.
            Maybe I'm a coward though.

My father drank too much at night,
I never spoke up out of fear
of starting a father-son fight.
I gave him money for his beer,
a lot of people knew it then
but I never asked him to know,
so I let it pass.
            Maybe I'm a coward though.

My brother found an awful lover,
she dragged him down a dark dream path.
One snowy night I yelled at her,
she went away but soon came back.
A lot of people knew it then
but I never asked him to know,
so I let it pass.
            Maybe I'm a coward though.

My love she says, *Why do you drink
too much and sometimes go and smoke?*
It's hard for me to stop and think
when I wish to drink and drift and float.
A lot of people know it now
but I don't ask myself to know,
so I let it pass.
            Maybe I'm a coward though.

Dark Days

It is always the stacking
of negative things
that teaches us new limits:
one hope dissipates, then another,
and another.

Grandma Bea had too many strokes
and had to give up her log home,
my favorite place.
Dad died;
Uncle Bruce got stage-four
throat cancer
and I tried not to hate my life,
stay thankful for something.

But my brother was living with
a drug-addict alcoholic,
now she sat at my Thanksgiving
table, the embodiment of every
negative force around:
twenty years of Thanksgivings
at Grandma Bea's, gone;
dad, gone; brother, gone;
but sitting there, still
trying to care for something that
only cares about itself,
I watched her fill up her plate
with my family's food, sucking
nourishment from anywhere,
sucking in any spirit my
brother had left.

They became dark days.
I cried a lot then;
leaves fell and I watered them.
I hoped those tears wouldn't
grow into anything worse
or poison any innocent tree.

I begged for my brother to come back,
for my uncle not to die.
It was my favorite time of year; but
I felt like the trees,
falling off,
falling down,
hit the ground
with my knees
to crunch leaves
and summon anything
spiritual to get through
the dying season.

Wrong or Right?

Heavily it weighs on my mind
to find my life a wreckage trail,
choice after choice until
I have found myself here
in the ashes of my decisions.

Alan Watts, the philosopher,
would say there are no wrong decisions,
Have you ever seen a misshapen cloud
or poorly designed wave? Of course not, it's nonsense.
And I think it must be true:
I have never seen a bee fly into the wrong flower
or a spider spin the wrong web.

Then again, Yeats, one afternoon
shouted into a pit, hearing his own echo
and talking back to it, troubled he would
lie awake night after night
and never get the answers right.
And I think it must be true,
when my dad was too drunk he would light
a cigarette the wrong way round,
after two drags smoking the filter end fumes
he would realize his mistake,
God Dammit, Shit!
That must be a wrong decision.

I have faltered from my own self-destruction
too many times to know that when there are
moments of peace I enjoy them.

When asked at restaurants,
What would you like on that?

I say, *Everything.*

I say, *Everything*.
Every drunk disaster,
every misshapen decision,
poorly designed web,
every mile on an open road
with the windows down,
every beautiful day,
even if they are mostly gray,
every star that stole my stare,
every wave I've ever seen
that made a part of my mind sing.

There is no wrong, no right,

only being.

There is only us.

There is only everything.

A Night on a Train Window

I don't know that face that's
over mine, it seems old,
not in years, but in time spent.
It stares back, through me
and I stare through it,
floating on a night-train window.

I focus on the whites of his eyes
to not see the black of them
and wish I had another drink, so
I could forgive, forget the world
flicking past, through
my translucent face, printed smears
of distorted sweeping concrete
and light, black air and purple
silhouetted trees, missing fields
with broken flowers after heavy rain,
and litter angels picking up
what they can find on the streets.

It goes by so fast.
I don't talk to you anymore,
you are in the past
and I cannot get there.

Am I the train or the dark air,
the seat or the glass,
those eyes or the sadness
of that translucent mess?

Am I the past tracks,
or am the next?

Shut Down

When we shut down
for winter or longer
we do not give a last
burst of color to the world.

When you shut down one autumn,
even the maples tried to save you,
swirled their radiating leaf-glow
around you to prop you up,
make you smile,
but they ran out of time.

Winter came, and by
blooming spring you were
dancing with skeletons
and not even the cherry
blossoms could make
you smile again.

Trapped Sparrow

That year I only saved one thing,
a sparrow caught on fishing string;
in its nest it spun around
in panicked circles above the ground.

I looked around, I looked around
to see my friends all on the ground
to see my dad in dying steps
to see sad truth I'd soon forget
to see my brother crawling low
under the light, burnt and slow.

Desperate to stay myself
I needed to save something else,
I cupped the little sparrow close,
I cut the string and gave him hope
to fly again as a real bird
and hoped his flapping wings were heard
by anyone or anything,
that bird my only song to sing.

Coffee

Coffee is a good thing.
I learned to drink it too young, with Gramps
who would wake too early
to watch frost with a hanging head.
A deep sadness is carried
by men who often spread cheer themselves
but know the grim realities of life;
it stays with those who have love in their hearts despite
the darkness of the world.

I let an early frost-covered weekend morning break the silence,
and watch the cold glisten outside the kitchen window.
The house is asleep, I am not.
My head hangs, my heart hangs,
my thoughts aren't of anything memorable or meaningful.

Slow mornings are good.
I wish I could share them with Gramps and Dad.
I say *bring the season on* with a quiet passion.
Dying colors have that special beauty,
an irreplaceable hit on the senses.
The air is cold, the coffee hot,
and I somewhere in between.
If anything, I am ahead of the day,
but behind in everything else,
thinking on this autumn morning.

Rising Early

Gramps woke up early
to drink coffee
old farmer hours
before the day's
work began.

He designed that house
for Grandma Bea and him;
he wanted three things:
a stone fireplace,
a two-car garage,
and a large basement;
he had them all, out
in the rolling green
mountains on a hilltop.
There aren't many
better places
to wake up.

I would sneak out
early as a boy to
see him at the table,
ask him for the same
coffee he had and pretend
that I knew about
manly things.

We would talk nature,
the woods, the bear that
stopped by sometimes,
his childhood farm,
our love of dogs.

He would tell me the
raisins in my oatmeal
were deer droppings
from the woods,
referred to as
'deer raisins.'

As I grew up we would
still have our coffee
breaks discussing the
same things but also,
now, girls, about the loss
of his first wife,
about his three years
as a prisoner of war.
These events tortured him;
I saw how his head hung
in his chair when it was
too quiet; I noticed there
was always a moment when
I showed up for coffee breaks
before Gramps would notice
me: his head hung, lost
gazing eyes staring into
the depth of what was
behind him.

My coffee this morning
reminded me of all that,
the sky blue as it deserves
to be, the crisp air that hit
my nose, floral scents,
mixed with coffee aroma.

My head hangs but I know
because of Gramps
there is no such thing
as an early coffee break alone.

Where My Father Stepped

I have known the path trodden
through forest floor dirt
where my father has stepped,
the woods in the east whose
leaves hold that warm green
golden light of summer,
whose forest rivers,
clear and bronze,
cast down through smooth stones,
cut through steep hills,
and hold his best footprints,
where my father stepped and left
parts of his heart on young hearts.

I have known the tragedy
of his bravery after war,
muddy jungle rotting steps
he took far from home
to watch friends step
their last steps
to watch friends gasp
their last breaths.

I have known his last steps,
those shuffling struggling sickness steps
and the march of Marine brethren
who carried him his final steps,
those were his feet
and his feet those
marching, linked by spirit breaths,
the fate some soldiers chose.

He has known my first steps in a
humbling father's joy to see an
early life after taking lives,
thanking God my guns were toys.

I know now he steps where I step,
just ahead or just behind;
our earthly wrongs matter not;
even though he has left
I have known where
my father stepped.

Sad Eyes

you with those full   sad eyes

there is nothing I can do   for you

except remind you life is   full of color

especially now   before winter

to be sad now is   a wasted autumn

to not feel the hit   on the senses

to waste even one day   of this

with those deep   sad eyes

is to be dead already

    but there is healing power   even in the blacks

    of your eyes

    that hold a slight glisten

    of golden glow

    in an evening

holding the small warmth   that may be the thing

    that saves your life.

Last Light

Few men say farewell like
in the old times
but the boys built a fire
for you, put on their
songs and skits,
let you speak to end
the evening.

We all knew it was
your last fire,
your last light,
and to see you,
my father, brother,
speaking to the boys as
an orange-glowing silhouette
with dancing words,
bright, whipping flames,
to tell them their lives
were great, their lives
would be full of the most
unexpected, full of wonder
and of where the smoke goes to,
into the tops of faintly lit
night time summer treetops,
where no one can see, staring
far into the unknown, the spirit world,

and I was proud to have shared all
this with you,
the last light of a fire,
of a man
who warmed the hearts of many.

Twenty-One Shots

On a blue October day twenty-one shots
echoed through my heart,
jolted me back into the current moment
where my thoughts had wandered,
back to Pop-Pop's firing salute years before;
this time empty shells hit the ground
and heavy blasts hit the air for my father.

Warriors get what they deserve at Arlington,
where their heavy hearts can rest.
Left here with our troubled hearts.
Rest well and forever;
everything that life has taken
from you has been given back.

Have you ever seen Marines fold a flag?
I'll only see it once:
Marines in perfect symmetry,
folding the flag over my father,
ceremonial, sad, perfect,
brothers honoring each other
separated only by time.

I've had family in every American war.
Dad said he went to war so
Kevin and I did not have to.

God, I hope I deserve not
to see combat. I hope all
their blood has been enough.
God, I hope I live well enough
knowing there is a burden
they carried that I will
never be able to repay.

For Them

From there I could see the memories
hung on monuments of wars and
songs sung at ceremonies
of dead parents and grandparents,
stories of their parents and grandparents.
Etched stone names remain,
or marble or wooden plaques, lonely
town statues that remember someone
important, and I know my father is
etched in stone for brave reasons and
when I walk around that place the madness
in the world feels at peace, and though it is
the reason for it, when I'm there, war seems
like a faraway place that cannot touch you.

Black Breath

The interior of your house
charred from the vapors
your breath fumed,
like barrels burnt on the inside
that held your whisky.

Charming as you were,
a boozy aroma entered
a room before your false
words ever could.

The holiday home crumbles,
burnt on the inside:
a rusty stone shell of
hollow memories.

No one goes there,
like your gravesite
crumbling low in
overgrown grass.

As they danced and lived
in your charred playground,
they got covered in ash.
You ran off to die alone,
left them like everything
that came across your
black breath,

      burnt on the inside,
      ready to crumble.

Observing Autumn

People who try to meditate are amusing,
like it can be scheduled into the day to
attain peace of mind before going back
to life chores.

I finally discovered that I was not important,
so my troubles were also not important,
my stresses, thoughts, feelings,
even my life, to an extent.
I began to truly observe.

Few sit back as I do now,
never offended because I know
it is all funny and weird,
joyful and completely fucked up,
this, my favorite season.

I can wait for frost with coffee,
or red wine, or beer, or bourbon,
watch colors that paintbrushes
can't quite recreate
slowly drift along
in the breeze,
see the world arguing with itself
as all the people in it claim importance,
while I get to sit back
and observe autumn.

Spilled Out on a Wall

I enter a house of things
that used to be a favorite place,
but seasons change,
people leave,
drift away as autumn leaves,
human clutter left
in stacks for relatives
to sort and pack.

I scan the living room,
deciding which memory
or yours to empty next,
noticing all the intricate
details I missed before,

I grabbed that large painting,
tilting it towards me.
Towering over my head,
a painting of a cabin within
this cabin, perched on a cliff
by a waterfall in a conifer forest,
deep and green and violent and peaceful.

As it lowered, I felt its pressure
release, spilling out of its frame
flowing down my arms,
crashing onto the organ
below, that no one played anymore,
roaring musical notes through the house,

rattling every wooden board,
filling up every room one last time
with one more joke-filled story,
one more gaze across
the mountains from the front porch,

flowing down the hill
filling up the pond
pushing out the little boat
for one last look at that thin
place sitting atop the hill,
or on a wall dreaming
by a raging waterfall
to keep this place as it once was,
drowning out these pointless words,
all of this spilled out on a wall.

Fall

Patrick Rheady McHale died
face-down in a gutter frozen
in Philadelphia.

I've woken up in a gutter
in the rain, four
generations later.
Luckily for me it was
early fall,
too warm to freeze
to death.

Any uncle, father,
brother, or grandfather
woke up in similar places.

Drinking like that doesn't
always give a second chance.

Autumn sounds better
but fall is closer
to the truth.

Oak Leaves

Oak leaves are falling gently,
hitting glass, fluttering off the roof
like paper skipping along
a river, like the deliberate
way we wrap presents,
marked, like each leaf
with our unique prints
and best intentions.

All of it a gift, bundles
of them raked into piles
for us to dive into,
throw in the air,
remember what youth
smelled like after the cutting
of the hay in late summer,

there isn't much else here,
what else would there
ever need to be?

Real Air

I hold out my hand
for any living thing
to take it,
land on it,
eat out of it:
a bird,
a butterfly,
sing or dance on it,

or you to take it with
a real human hand
to run off somewhere
in a sun-rain-kissed
valley that bends light
in surreal ways.

So a breeze that is you
takes my hand across
the dancing light
landscape where
everything seems
to actually live.

Another Day

I thought about driving straight
past this damned place this morning,
head west or north,
find a cliff or coast,
a loch with conifers around it,
stare into its lost deep blue,

or find an old stone Highland house
that people once called their own,
any village or small town with
bent beams by an open fire in a pub
with a local man to discuss life with.

It's getting colder, darker.
I question the tie I'm wearing,
the suit, the stress.
Over the horizon I see meadows
and tree lines holding back
the first chilly rays of warmth.

Alone in the car
my isolated soul
knowing how to be
but trapped on
how to go.

The Trail

You took a turn we are all
afraid to take, turned right and
went west instead of driving
south to work, you left behind
the things that make life heavy:
wallet, phone, keys, passport.
You struggle in these modern
times, as you know these items
are not who we are.

You parked somewhere along
the Appalachian Trail and started walking,
in our world; you went missing, alerts
went up, people worried, I was
worried too, old friend,
but now I wish I was on the trail with you.

You'd been sighted in a small town
somewhere in Virginia;
word had it you'd already been
given your trail name, 'Bear Strayer.'

I smiled when I heard the report of an
enormous man carrying nothing but
a ground cloth: a straying bear,
not a lost bear, not a worried bear,
a bear as it should be, roaming free.

Back in Scouts in the Order of the Arrow
we performed Indian ceremonies in firelight,
we did our best with the spirit world
as imposters dressed as natives,
that natural world you have returned to.

You helped pick my Indian name:
Wulantawagon –
He who has good spirits.
But that was before I knew the world
was heavy, before my pockets were
weighed down with those heavy things:
wallet, phone, keys, passport.

I'd like to think I could find you on the trail,
join in on your adventures,
turn right and head west
instead of south to work;
we could be missing together,
when the truth is, everyone else
seems to be lost; but out there,
Bear Strayer, on the trail,
every missing thing
seems to be found.

Old Pier

Something worth knowing about an old pier
where fisherman go year after year: it hears
their jokes, keeps their stories safely deep in wooden posts,
where wisdom stays to grow in clusters of shelled creatures,
exposed at low tide, the ebb and flow,
listening and letting go.

It shifts its boards for the visitors who walk on it:
the old man who walks it every morning to think,
drink coffee and hope his time on earth has been worthwhile,
to listen to seabirds and to nothing.

The old pier knows this old man,
it bends under his heavy foot
its boards creak a little louder
to take some aches out of the old man's bones.

But for the young, adolescent, two-week summer romance,
laughing, light, ice-cream and kisses, the boards lighten,
spring their youthful feet back up to propel them into life.

For me, alone, I went out to the end, where
my land-loving feet had to stop.
A low line of cumulus horse heads and chariots
raced from right to left, into nothing, into everything,

I wished to join them, I wished to become stuck
to the posts, a snail, a barnacle, or a statue at piers end
to not miss the chariot race ever again,
to always be in the spray,
to always know young love in summer and old solitude in winter,
all of it from one spot, like a tree's wisdom kept in sand,

wise as one hundred trees shaped into posts and boards,
a forest of knowledge hidden, unseen,
deep in wooden rings and rusty nails
known at the edge,
always between the spray
and that old pier.

The Weather

I check the forecast of where you are,
check the weather of everywhere I've been,
know that I have a piece of each place
the way it was once.

I check to know when it
rains on you
or snows,
or worse,

and I am filled with tiny
impulses of delight
when I know the sun
is shining on you,

or anywhere I have been,
and I can imagine
what you might
be doing.

Cretan Hilde

You collect seaside things to make crafts,
spend days strolling the sand
picking up shells,
knowing the driftwood you find is like you,
it ran away from some other place
and is happy to be in Crete.

We crave the forgotten things
on the beach which are like us,
we need waves
or a riverbank
or a lakeside
to pulse with the rhythm of the water,
the lapping of the waves,
the crashing and the letting go,

so a brush forces you to pick it up
and capture Cretan colors,

Poseidon always lured you in to some
Greek dream by the sea and the Muses
sealed your fate on an island
and you are at peace with your new
dream world.

Home is Crete now,
it has always been home.

Happiness is not a destination
but for you it was,
not in some Belgian field
but the morning you
realized you had never even
lived until you became
Cretan Hilde.

This Night

People should sit out
here at this time but
I'm glad they don't.

I am content with the
nothingness I am,
with this night I
will never be,
with its normal,
simple majesty.

A black shimmering pond
under an outlined weeping willow,
slightly distorted as
people who you don't quite
know have more depth
in their lack of detail;
that slivered moon and
how it warps the light it steals
around the clouds it does not know,
seen by people it does not know
or care about.

Some sky artist hangs in space,
looks down,
paints,
adds a star every now and then.

The north star appears
but I am as far north as
I ever need to go
and people in their little houses

in little rooms, fixed to
little glowing screens,
leave this little spot
for me at night.

I do not know if I have
been painted in the
wrong place;
on this night,
I do not need
to know.

Out to the Blue Ridge

I took a friend's truck out to
the Blue Ridge in early winter light.

I let the engine slowly roar
down Skyline Drive
absorbed into the cold smoky
blue of those mountains,
them and I in our best winter light.

I forgot how quiet it all is.
I hiked up Mount Marshall,
saw the blue-tinged landscape
the winter-blanket-clouds
saw the seconds strung out to minutes,
frozen hikers' footprints in the ground,
how they would thaw and go
like any imprint we make in this life,
here and gone.

Content in all that remains unseen,
those who whispered here once
who passed by on foot, on horseback,
by car, by chance

everyone needing to see this
one at a time

like how good friendships are made
one at a time

how mountains are crafted
one at a time

how any life must be lived
one at a time

I'll give you this truck,
my friend won't mind,
he'd want you to drive out here alone
as I would,
wind down the Shenandoahs
to your own mountain song.

I only request you pass the keys
along when you are done
so that, alive or long dead,
or on foot or
on horseback
or without knowing each other,
we have all shared this open road
one at a time,

leaving only
our frail
fading imprints
in the time
we were given.

Frost Covered

Up early when
frost breaks in lower angled light
and morning fields look
blessed by frozen silver,
at least a hundred birds awake,
vocal, cheerful, conversing
about some secret I could
never know,
giggling as they flutter
around each other
behind the colors
of the remaining leaves
that would soon be gone,
they would all soon be gone.

That lovely screen
drops away to bareness,
contorted wooden bones,
nothing to distract from the
stripped down things we become,
the nakedness,
the 'what we once were'
when all there is
is still
and covered
in a frozen
dust

Never Having Been Here

If I sat here forever on this hillside
and rotted with this bench
like an old stump,
would people know
I had ever been here?

What do people know?

They keep trying to build statues
out of stone and bronze and steel
to rot away like a stump,
moss covered and forgotten.

If you stay longer than me
and I am a stump,
as we all become
a fallen tree,
I will tell stories to the air,
hope birds hear them and
carry them to you,
lightly sing them to you
in a voice more pleasant
than my own,
give you directions
to come sit by me
on that bench.

It may be painful to
know I have become
forgotten air,

But worse, if we loved
never having been here.

Kyle McHale is originally from the suburbs of Washington D.C. in Maryland. He currently lives and works in Surrey, England. This is his first published collection of poems, though he has been reading and writing poetry for over a decade.